HOW WE BUILD

DAMS

HOW WE BUILD

DAMS

Neil Ardley

GEC GARRETT EDUCATIONAL CORPORATION

© GEC Garrett Educational Corporation

Edited by Rebecca Stefoff

U.S.A. text © 1990 by Garrett Educational Corporation
First Published in the United States in 1990 by
Garrett Educational Corporation, 130 East 13th Street,
Ada, OK 74820

First Published 1989 by Macmillan Children's Books,
England, © Macmillan Publishers Limited 1989

Manufactured in the United States of America

Library of Congress Cataloging-in-Publication Data

Ardley, Neil.
    Dams / Neil Ardley.
      p. cm. - (How we build)
    Includes index.
    Summary: Describes the construction and use of dams and discusses
their benefits and dangers.
    ISBN 0-944483-75-5
    1. Dams-Design and construction-Juvenile literature. 2. Dams-Juvenile
literature. [1. Dams-Design and construction. 2. Dams.] I. Title II. Series.
TC540.A73   1990
627'.8-dc20   90-40360
                                                 CIP
                                                 AC

Note to the reader
In this book there are some words in the text which are printed in **bold** type.
This shows that the word is listed in the glossary on page 46. The glossary
gives a brief explanation of words that may be new to you.

Contents

Collecting and storing water

Water is a precious substance. We cannot live without it. We must have water for drinking and for cooking our food. We need water for washing our bodies and our clothes, for keeping our homes clean, and for making our gardens grow.

Most of us are fortunate. We turn on the tap and as much clear, clean water as we want comes out. The supply seems endless. It is not like that for everyone.

Water from the sky

The water that comes out of the tap begins its journey as drops of rain. The rain flows over the land or under the ground to fill the lakes and rivers. In very dry countries, however, or in times of drought, the level of water in the lakes and rivers falls. The lakes and rivers may even dry up. Then people have to use whatever water there is very carefully and not waste a drop.

River barriers

The **water authorities** have the job of collecting and storing water from the rivers and lakes. Often they build dams to make sure that there is enough water no matter how much or how little rain there may be.

A dam is a barrier built across a river to stop the water from flowing freely. The water collects and rises behind the dam to form a lake. This type of artificial lake is called a **reservoir.**

A reservoir holds some of the water flowing in the river in reserve, so that it can be used at times when there is a shortage of rain. The water in the reservoir is used by the water authorities. They purify it to make it clean for people to drink. After it is purified, the water is stored in huge tanks until it is needed. Then the water is piped from the storage tanks to the water tanks and taps in our homes.

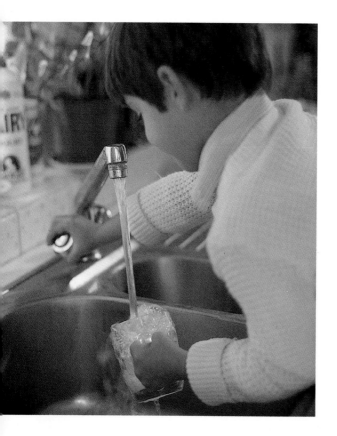

◄ Most of us run water from the tap without thinking twice about it. To bring water to your home, engineers have had to lay pipes and build tanks and reservoirs. They may have had to build dams to control the supply of water.

► Villagers draw water from the communal well. Many people still rely on wells for all their drinking water and often for washing themselves and their clothes too.

▲ Building work on the Victoria Dam is Sri Lanka was completed in 1984. Not only does it provide water for crops, but the power of the falling water is also used to make electricity.

Shortage of water

Dams and reservoirs are particularly important in areas where there is little rainfall. However, they are expensive to build, so not every country can afford them. In some areas, people have to collect their water from village wells or from streams or rivers.

Dam building

In this book you will learn why certain types of dams are built. We shall also find out what problems **engineers** have to solve in order to build the dams and keep the water flowing.

Supply and control

Dams and reservoirs do not only supply water for domestic use. Water is also needed for industry and farming, and as a source of power. All of these take large amounts of water.

Water in industry

Water goes into canned and preserved food. It is mixed with wood pulp to make paper. The process of making gasoline from crude oil uses ten times more water than the amount of gasoline that is made.

▼ Water is essential for most industries. Here, in a papermaking factory, they use as much water every day as the people of a small city.

Water for crops

Plants cannot grow without water. If there is not enough rain during the growing season, farmers have to find other ways of watering their crops. They may **irrigate** their crops by digging channels in the ground to a river or lake, so that the water can flow through the channels to their fields. Dams may be built to keep water in reserve until it is needed by the farmers.

Water for power

Sometimes dams and reservoirs are built to provide water for **power stations.** The movement of fast-flowing water through a dam produces energy which can be turned into electricity. Electricity made in this way is called **hydroelectric power,** from the Greek work *hydor,* meaning water.

Flood control

A dam does not only store water, it also controls the amount of water that flows through it. After a heavy rainfall, rivers may overflow. Sometimes they burst their banks and cause floods that wash away whole towns, drowning people and their livestock. Disasters of this kind can be prevented by damming rivers, so that the lakes and rivers below the dam will no longer rise high enough to flood.

Sometimes, a river floods its banks because of high tides rushing in from the sea. In recent years, **flood barriers** have been built to hold back the incoming tides.

◄ Irrigation ditches have been dug to carry water from the canal to the crops. Without the water, crops could not be grown in this dry part of Arizona.

An irrigation experiment

You will need: a large plastic tray, a pile of garden soil, and a bucket of water.

1 Take the tray outside and lay it on a flat surface. Fill it with dry soil.

2 The picture shows you how to shape the soil to make a reservoir at one end and two ditches, or irrigation channels, along the length of the tray.

3 Fill the reservoir with water, so that the water enters the irrigation channels.

4 What happens to the soil? What happens to the water? How does it irrigate the land?

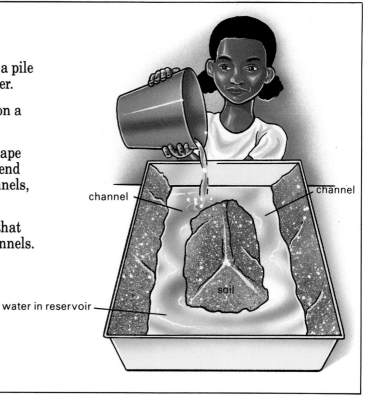

channel

channel

soil

water in reservoir

Dams in history

The first dams we know of were built for the irrigation of crops. They were made by piling up banks of earth or by building barriers of wood and reeds. Some were made with rocks and stone. A dam constructed out of earth and stone more than 5000 years ago has been found in Jordan, in the Middle East.

Damming the Nile River

The ancient Egyptians were skilled engineers. Their vast pyramids, which still stand just outside the city of Cairo, were built about 2600 BC.

At about the same time, the Egyptians built an enormous dam across the Nile River. Its remains can be seen today at Sadd el-Kafara, 20 miles (32 kilometers) south of Cairo. The dam was built in order to make a lake, and the water collected was used for work in a nearby quarry. The dam was 36 feet (11 meters) high and 348 feet (106 meters) long. Its base was 276 feet (84 meters wide). The dam was constructed of two walls of rocks, with gravel filling the space in between. It did not last as long as the pyramids, however. Soon after it was built, the central section of the dam was washed away by floods.

Roman dams

The Romans constructed many fine roads and bridges in the countries they conquered. Some of these dams still stand. About 2000 years ago, the Romans built two dams near the town of Merida, in Spain, to provide water for the town. They were built so well that they are still used to provide water for irrigation.

▼ Beavers can gnaw through tree trunks that are nearly two feet thick. The fallen tree creates a natural dam in a river or a stream. Any gaps are filled with mud, stones or leaves.

Stronger dams

About 400 years ago, dam builders in Spain discovered that a curved dam is much stronger than a straight dam and can be built much higher. The Tibi Dam, on the Monegre River near Alicante, is an **arch dam.** It is curved like an archway laid flat, with the top of the curve pointing upstream. It was built in 1589, and remained the highest dam in the world for almost 300 years. It is still used for irrigation.

During the 1800s, engineers learned more about how to make dams strong enough to withstand the immense power of running water. Using the new machinery which was being invented at that time, they began to build larger and higher dams. In the last hundred years, enormous dams have been built all over the world, often in remote places where the construction was extremely difficult.

▲ The Nile River was the Egyptians' only source of water so they had to find ways of ensuring the people and their crops had enough water. Dams were built to store the water.

▼ The Meer Alum Dam near Hyderabad in India. This dam was completed in 1802.

Where to build

The first thing engineers need to know, before they can even choose the site for a dam, is the reason why it is to be built. If the dam is to supply water, it should be built in a place where a large reservoir can be formed. If the dam is to provide power, it may have to be high up in the mountains, where the water falls downward with plenty of force. The dams may be a long way from the places where the water and electricity are needed. Pipelines will take the water to the cities and towns. The electricity created can be sent through cables.

Choosing a valley

To find the best site, engineers study maps that show where rivers and streams flow through valleys between hills or mountains. If there are steep slopes on both sides of the valley, it can be dammed to make a reservoir.

Having chosen a site for the dam, the engineers go there to **survey** the valley. They can estimate, from its size and shape, the amount of water flowing into it. From the measurements they take, they can work out how big the reservoir will be when the dam is finished. It is essential to know exactly how much water there will be in the reservoir, so that the dam can be made strong enough to hold back the water without breaking.

▶ Before a dam is built, engineers measure the land and make a detailed map of the area. They must find out how much water flows through the valley at different times of the year.

Soil and rock

Before engineers can make the final decision to build a dam, they need to know more about the composition of the soil and rock at the site where the dam is to be built. The soil and rock base has to be firm and strong enough to support the weight of the dam. They also have to make sure the reservoir will be watertight. To obtain this information, the engineers need the expert advice of **geologists.**

The geologists bore holes in the floor and walls of the valley to take soil and rock samples. The samples are tested in a laboratory to measure the strength of the soil and rock to find out whether or not water passes through them easily. The geologists may have to dig shafts and tunnels into the ground to take a closer look.

The engineers must make sure that the soil and rock will not move once the dam is built and the reservoir has formed. Otherwise, the dam could give way and flood the whole area.

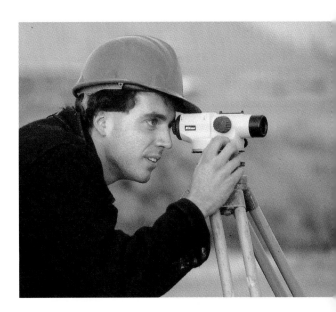

▲ Geologists have to investigate the chosen site before a dam can be built. They take samples to study the rock of the floor and walls of a valley.

▼ In 1965, there were many protest marches by local people about the plans to build the Tryweryn Dam in Wales. This was because many of their houses and farms were to be covered with water when the dam was completed.

People and dams

The valley chosen for the dam may be geologically suitable, but there may be people living and working there. The government must consider them before deciding to build the dam. If the dam is built, these people will have to be relocated because their homes and farms will be drowned as the water level rises. In 1987, the Indian government reconsidered its plan to build dams in the Namada Valley when it realized that more than a million people, from 435 villages and one large town, would have to be relocated.

Planning a dam

Before they can build on the chosen site, engineers must design the dam with great care and work out the cost. Their plans must show the exact shape and size of the dam and what materials are to be used.

The design of every dam is different. Each design depends upon how high and how wide the valley is and on the soil and rock found there.

▼ The design of one dam may be very different from the design of another. An embankment dam is massive and has sloping sides. A concrete dam is tall and narrow.

Types of dam

There are two main types of dam. An **embankment dam** is a hugh pile of soil or rock. The great weight of the dam keeps it in place, so that it holds back the water behind it. Dam builders choose this type of dam when the valley is wide and shallow, and when the rock in the walls of the valley is not hard enough to support the weight of a concrete dam.

A **concrete dam** is the type most often built when the valley is deep and narrow. A concrete dam can be tall and thin-walled yet very strong. However, the rock in the floor and walls of the valley must be hard, so that it will help to support the base and sides of the dam.

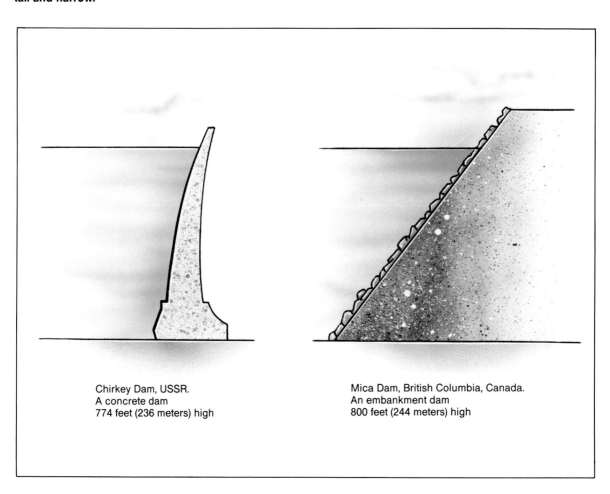

Chirkey Dam, USSR.
A concrete dam
774 feet (236 meters) high

Mica Dam, British Columbia, Canada.
An embankment dam
800 feet (244 meters) high

The strength of the dam

Engineers who design a dam use
computers to help them to calculate the
forces that will exert pressure upon the
dam. These forces include the weight of
the water that will push against the dam
and the force with which the dam and the
sides of the valley will push back against
the water. The strength of the finished
dam will be determined by these forces.
All the forces acting together make the
dam stay in place.

▲ Engineers use models of dams and flood barriers
to determine how the real dam will stand up to the
force of the water.

Engineers are continually measuring
the forces that are exerted on dams that
have already been built and the strength
of these dams. This helps engineers who
are designing a new dam to estimate how
strong it will be. Detailed drawings and
scale models of the proposed dam are
prepared.

A watertight barrier

An embankment dam forms a massive barrier across a valley. The front of the dam slopes down to the bottom of the valley, and it is covered with grass or bare rock. Often there is a road along the top of the dam. On the other side of the dam, the water rises almost to the top.

Sloping sides

If you could see the whole embankment dam without the water, you would see a wall of soil or rock shaped like an enormous triangle. Both sides of the dam slope outwards from the top. The dam is built in a triangular shape so that it is thickest at its base, where the pressure of water against the dam is greatest.

The side that is under the water is often covered with rocks or stones, which protect the dam. Without this cover, waves would beat against the dam and tear away the soil.

Inside the dam

An embankment dam is not naturally watertight. Water can seep through the soil and rock that form the dam. It can also seep through the ground under the dam. Seeping water can weaken the dam and could make it give way.

Therefore, embankment dams contain a **core.** The core is a barrier placed inside the dam to stop water from seeping through. Often it is made of clay, which does not absorb water.

Underneath the dam, there may be another barrier, called a **cut-off** or curtain, to stop water from getting through. The cut-off goes down into the ground until it reaches hard rock, so it may be very deep. Usually it is made of clay or concrete.

Preventing a flood

Usually, there is a wide channel called a **spillway** at the side of an embankment dam. If the water in the reservoir becomes too high, water overflows into the spillway and, through it, down into the valley.

The spillway keeps the reservoir at a safe level and prevents the water in the reservoir from flooding over the top of the dam. If that happened, the water would tear away the soil or rock in the dam, and the dam would collapse.

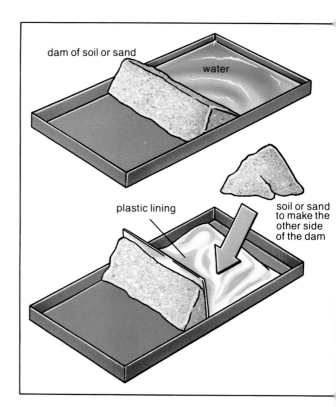

dam of soil or sand

water

plastic lining

soil or sand to make the other side of the dam

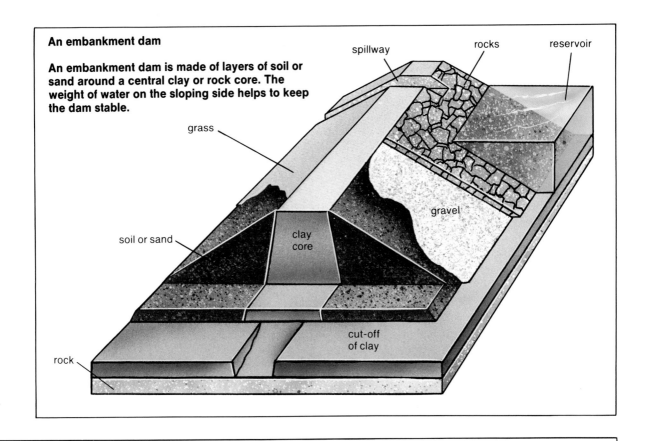

An embankment dam

An embankment dam is made of layers of soil or sand around a central clay or rock core. The weight of water on the sloping side helps to keep the dam stable.

Labels: spillway, rocks, reservoir, grass, gravel, soil or sand, clay core, cut-off of clay, rock

Make an embankment dam

You will need: a large plastic tray, some soil or sand, water, and a plastic bag.

1 Take the tray outside. Lay it on a flat surface. Shape the soil or sand into a firm dam across the middle of the tray.

2 Fill the tray with water on one side of the dam. Watch what happens. How long does it take for the water to leak through the sides and under the dam?

3 Now pour away the water and rebuild the dam. Look at the picture to see how to put the plastic bag in the middle of the dam, so that it acts like a clay core in a real dam.

4 Repeat the experiment. What happens when you pour in the water? How long does it take for the water to leak through the dam this time?

A dry site

Once the government has given permission for a new dam to be built, the work of preparing the site for construction can begin. The builders of the dam assemble all the people, machines and materials that they will need to do the job. Building a dam is a very big enterprise that takes several years.

Preparing the site

The first task that faces the builders of an embankment dam is to prevent the river from flowing through the site

▼ A cofferdam is a type of barrier which diverts the river while the dam is being built. After the area behind the cofferdam has been pumped dry, work can begin on the exposed river bed.

where people will be working. To do this, the engineers construct a low dam called a **cofferdam** across the river. The cofferdam diverts the river and keeps the site dry.

The builders also dig a tunnel through the rock on one side of the valley. As the water in the river rises behind the cofferdam, it flows along the tunnel to the other end of the site. There, it spills back into the valley and becomes a river once more.

The cofferdam may be removed when the embankment dam is completed. Often, however, the dam is built over the cofferdam so that the cofferdam becomes part of the embankment dam. The tunnel may be used to carry water from the reservoir when the dam is in use. It may channel water to a hydroelectric power station, or supply irrigation projects.

A cofferdam

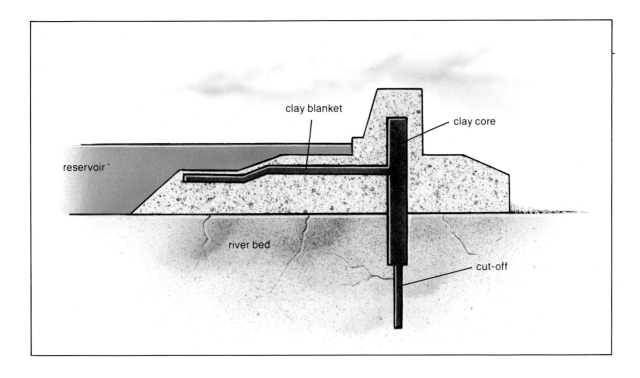

clay blanket

clay core

reservoir

river bed

cut-off

Digging down

Once the river has been diverted and the site is dry enough to work on, the dam builders start on the next stage of construction. If the ground is made of soil, sand, loose stones, or cracked rock, they will have to dig a trench across the valley. Huge excavators dig down until they reach hard, solid rock.

The builders fill the trench with clay, cement, or concrete to form the cut-off beneath the dam itself. Sometimes the depth of the cut-off is even greater than the height of the dam. However, if the valley floor is composed of hard rock, a cut-off may not be needed.

If the dam builders expect a lot of water to seep down through the dam to its base, they will build a layer of clay or concrete on the ground to prevent it from collecting under the dam. They may also dig channels in the ground to divert the water away from the base of the dam.

▲ The Aswan High Dam is in Egypt on the Nile River. It has a blanket and core of clay and a deep cut-off of clay and cement. These stop water from seeping through.

▼ The huge embankment dams built today rely on heavy machinery to do the hard work.

Layers of soil

With the site well prepared, the dam itself can be built up. An embankment dam can be made of soil, sand, gravel, stones, or large pieces of rock. The material used depends on the kind of soil or rock found in the vicinity. Usually, the dam builders dig up the material nearby and bring it to the site in dump trucks.

Building in soil or sand

A dam made of soil or sand is sometimes called an **earth dam.** It is built by piling layers of earth on top of each other until they reach the required height. Huge amounts of the material are needed to make the dam strong and solid. Many of the largest dams in the world are built using this method.

Once the central core is in place, bulldozers spread out the earth dumped by the trucks in even layers. Then powerful, very heavy rollers are driven over the layers to press them down and make the structure strong.

Sometimes the builders mix the earth with water and pump the mixture along pipes to the dam. As the water runs away, the earth settles in layers.

When the dam has reached its full height, the builders place a cover of stones or rocks on the side that will be under water. This is the **riprap.** It protects the dam from currents of water. The other side of the dam is sown with grass, because grass helps to hold the soil in the dam in position and prevent erosion.

▼ Construction work on the High Island Dam in Hong Kong. Heavy rollers drive backward and forward over each layer as it is laid. This ensures that the earth and stones are pressed tightly together and makes the embankment dam safe and strong.

A rock dam

If an embankment dam is built in a place where the land is rocky, it is likely to be made up of pieces of rock. This is called a **rockfill dam.** Because a rockfill dam is very strong and very heavy, it does not need to be as broad as an earth dam. The dam may have a core of clay, or a barrier of concrete may be laid over it on the underwater side. Either material will stop water from getting through the dam.

▶ Stone that has been quarried locally may be used to make a rockfill dam. This is the Marchlyn Dam and reservoir in North Wales before it was filled with water.

▼ The Mica Dam in Canada is an embankment dam built by the rockfill method.

Concrete dams

Very high concrete dams are often built in narrow valleys with steep sides. The high dams hold back deep reservoirs of water, yet the dams themselves can be very thin. Some of them are only ten feet (three meters) thick.

There are three main types of concrete dams: arch dams, **buttress dams,** and **gravity dams.** Some dams, such as arch-gravity dams, combine the features of two of the main types.

Curves of concrete

Tall, thin dams are built in a curved shape, or arch. The Tibi Dam, in Spain, was the first arch dam, built to curve into the reservoir. The shape of the arch dam makes the water press on the dam and push it against the sides of the valley. The dam is built to fit tightly between the floor and sides of the valley, so that it cannot move. Therefore, as the water pushes against the dam, it squeezes, or **compresses,** the concrete in the dam.

When concrete is compressed, it becomes very strong. This is why the dam does not burst. Some concrete dams curve not only into but also outward into the reservoir. These dams are called **cupola dams.** Their shape makes them very strong.

▶ Concrete dams are thinner than embankment dams. They can be given strength with a curved design, with supporting buttresses, or with the sheer weight of the concrete.

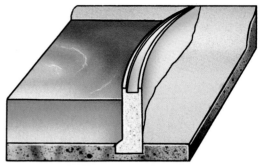
The curve of an arch dam spreads the weight of the water. The sides of the dam take the strain.

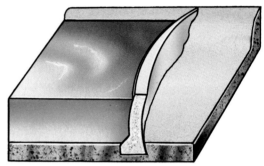
A cupola dam forms a round shell of concrete that is very strong.

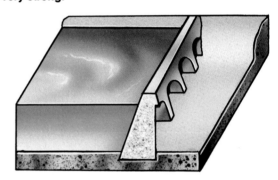
Buttresses are projecting walls that support the front of a dam.

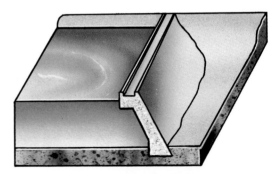
A gravity dam uses the weight of the concrete to hold back the water of the reservoir.

Straight barriers

Although the curve in the arch and cupola dams makes them strong, there are many straight concrete dams. However, these dams need buttresses to enable them to hold back the water in the reservoir. Buttress dams have triangular walls built against the side of the valley away from the water. Their triangular shape keeps them rigid. These buttresses hold the dam securely fixed to the valley floor and brace it so that it does not give way.

Safety in weight

A gravity dam is a huge, triangular block of concrete which is similar to the embankment dam in shape. However, the side facing the water is usually vertical, not sloping. Like an embankment dam, a gravity dam holds back the water because it is so heavy. Its great weight prevents it from giving way.

▼ The Couesque Dam is built into the side of a deep valley in France. It is designed as a cupola.

Building in sections

An embankment dam stretches across the whole valley and is built up from the ground, layer by layer. The construction is all part of one huge operation. Building a concrete dam is different. The dam can be constructed in sections, and one section can be completed before the next is begun. In addition, because concrete is hard and will not wash away, holes or tunnels can be made in the dam.

Therefore, when the builders prepare the site for a concrete dam, they do not have to divert the river around the whole site. The river continues to flow through one part of the site while construction workers are busy on another. As the work proceeds, the river may flow through a hole or tunnel in a completed section of the dam.

Working in water

The first thing the dam builders have to do is divert the river from the section of the site they plan to work on. They start by building the walls of the cofferdam out from one bank into the middle of the river. The cofferdam may be made of wood or steel and is in the shape of a large U rising above the surface of the water. When the water trapped inside the cofferdam has been pumped out, the river continues to flow around its walls,

Inside the cofferdam, the dam builders clear away the mud of the river bed and dig down to reach the hard rock beneath. They look for any cracks in the rock that might undermine the dam when it is built. They fill the

▼ A series of cofferdams allows a concrete dam to be built in sections. The river continues to flow through one section of the Victoria Dam in Sri Lanka while work begins on the next section.

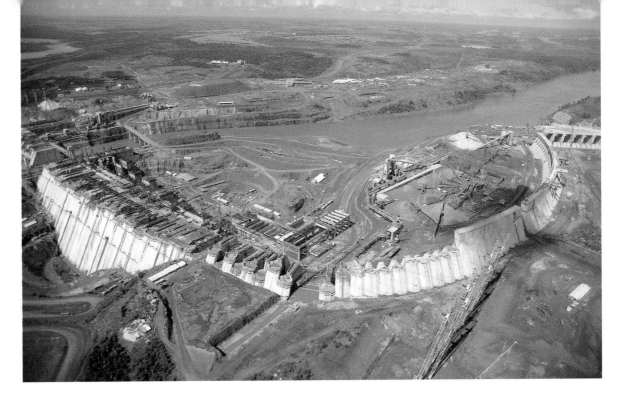

cracks with concrete to strengthen the rock and ensure that no water will seep under the dam.

▲ Huge sections of concrete rise across the construction site of the Itaipu Dam. Here, the waters of the Paraná River, in South America, have been diverted to one side of the site.

Underground support

Large structures, whether they are dams, skyscrapers, or bridges, need a firm foundation that goes down into the ground, supporting the weight of the structure and securing it to the ground.

Concrete dams need very strong foundations to support their weight and the great weight of water that pushes against them. Therefore, the base of the dam is built on a foundation of hard or strengthened rock.

An arch dam needs to be firmly attached to the rocky walls of the valley as well. Like the rock at the base, the rock on either side may need to be strengthened to support the dam. The side supports are called the **abutments** of the dam.

▲ The Gross Glockner Dam in Austria. Abutments have been added to the sides of this arch dam in order to give added support.

25

Pouring concrete

The first section of the dam is built on the rock foundation inside the cofferdam. This section is made with a channel or tunnel running through it. When the first section of the dam is complete, the builders remove the cofferdam and set it up in another part of the river. They can begin work on the next section of the dam inside the cofferdam, while the river flows through the channel or tunnel in the first section. The channel or tunnel may become a permanent part of the dam, or it may be sealed up when the dam is finished.

▼ Overhead buckets fill the forms with liquid concrete. This hardens into strong blocks that are then sealed with cement.

Working with concrete

Since concrete is a mixture of sand, gravel, broken stone, water, and cement, most of the materials can usually be found near the dam site. The liquid concrete is mixed at the side of the dam and is carried to the dam in buckets running over the site on cables.

The buckets pour the liquid concrete into **forms,** which are large open boxes made of wooden boards. The concrete sets inside the form to produce a concrete block. Then, the form is taken apart and set up alongside to make another block. This process is repeated until the dam is complete. Gaps between the blocks are sealed with cement.

Concrete gets warm when it sets, and overheating could cause it to crack, but building the dam in blocks allows the

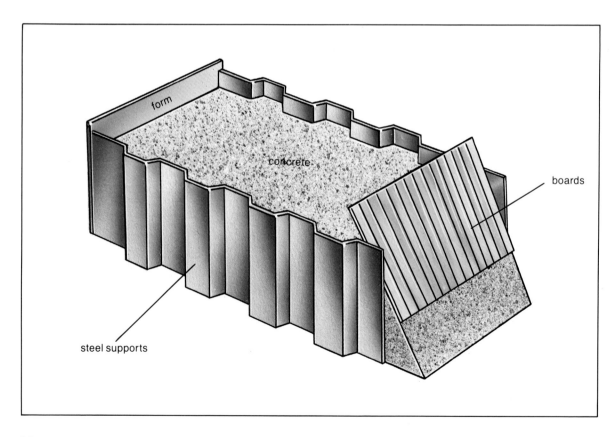

form

concrete

boards

steel supports

▲ The Daniel Johnson Dam is constructed from concrete blocks. It is sited on the Manicouagan River in Canada.

heat to escape. Each block is allowed to cool before other blocks are placed around it. Sometimes, pipes are inserted in the concrete and cold water pumped through them to speed up the process.

Strengthening concrete

It is possible to reduce the cost of building a dam by using less concrete. However, if that is done, the concrete used must be strengthened or **stressed.**

Stressing concrete has the same effect as compressing it. It adds strength. This is done by placing steel rods or cables inside the dam as it is built. The rods or cables run from the rock foundation to the top of the dam. Rods or cables also help to anchor the dam to its foundation. Stressing the concrete of a dam makes it possible to build a thin, straight dam without buttresses.

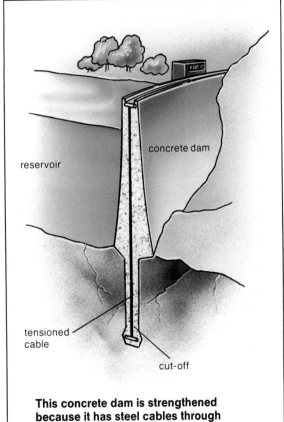

This concrete dam is strengthened because it has steel cables through the center.

Flowing water

When the dam is built, the water slowly rises behind it to form the reservoir. In many dams, the reservoir starts to form before the work on the dam is finished. Sometimes the water in it is used for generating power, or for irrigation, while work on the dam is still going on.

The dam does not merely hold water back. Every dam contains pipes, tunnels, or channels that have gates through which water can pass. The amount of water flowing through the dam can be controlled by these gates, so that there is always water for the people who need it.

▼ Sluices can be used to control huge volumes of water, as can be seen at the Kariba Dam on the Zambezi River in Africa.

▲ The spillway of the Itaipu Dam in South America.

Holes in the dam

If the tunnels that were built to divert the river during the dam's construction become permanent, they are equipped with gates which can be opened or closed. Dams may also contain large pipes or channels called **sluices,** which let water from the reservoir through the dam. Screens at the ends of the sluices prevent wood, leaves, and water plants from getting into them, while gates control the flow of water through them. The screens must be cleaned from time to time.

Some tall concrete dams let water through sluices high up in the dam. The water spurts out in great jets of spray, which then fall into the river valley below. These sluices stop the water from pounding down and wearing away the rock at the base of the dam.

Water for the river

Not all the water that passes through a dam is used for a specific purpose. Often, water is allowed through in order to keep the river in the valley below from drying up. Sometimes the dam is used to hold back floodwater and then release it slowly, so that the river does not overflow its banks.

Controlling the water level

By using the sluices, engineers control the level of water in the reservoir. How high that level should be depends upon how the dam is used. For irrigation purposes, the reservoir must fill up in wet seasons of the year so that there will be plenty of water for use during the dry season. Reservoirs supplying water to towns or power stations have to be kept full all the time.

Embankment dams have a spillway down the side of the dam to carry away surplus water. In other dams, the spillway is a large pipe that opens just above the required level of the water in the reservoir. Water flows into the spillway if the water level rises, and is carried down through the dam into the valley below.

Water from reservoirs

Like many people, you may rely on a dam and the reservoir behind it for your water supply. However, the water that flows out of your taps has to be treated before it is suitable for drinking.

Storing the water

It is not always necessary to build a dam to ensure a supply of water. Some of the water that we use comes from lakes or is pumped up from under the ground. Water can also be taken directly from rivers, without a dam being built to store the water. However, it does not come straight to us. The water is first pumped along pipes into reservoirs that are formed by building high walls of soil to contain the water.

The reservoirs store the water, so that, if the lake or river dries up, water can still be supplied to our homes. Both walled and dammed reservoirs help to purify the water they collect. When the water goes into a reservoir, it contains particles of soil. The water in the reservoir is so calm that the larger bits of soil settle slowly to the bottom.

Treating the water

The water that leaves the reservoir is cleaner than when it came in, but it needs further treatment before it is safe to drink. It still contains tiny particles of soil, and there may be germs that cause diseases. The water is therefore pumped to tanks in a water treatment plant, where **chemicals** are added to it. Some chemicals make the soil particles stick together and form lumps that then settle on the bottom of the tank. Other chemicals destroy whatever harmful germs there may be in the water.

The water also flows through **filters,** which strain off any remaining impurities. Often, the filters contain layers of sand. The grains of sand let the water through, but strain off the dirt particles.

Getting water into homes

When the water is clean and safe to drink, it is pumped from the treatment plant to large storage tanks. These tanks are kept full, so that they can provide water at any time. From the tanks, pipes carry the water under the ground and beneath the streets to our homes. If the storage tank is built high above the ground, the water will flow along the pipes without any need for pumps.

Tall water towers containing large storage tanks that supply water using this method can often be seen in towns and cities.

▼ The pipe that brings water to your home is called a water main. It is laid in an underground trench. Smaller pipes lead from the main to the house.

Rain falling on hills and mountains drains down into the reservoir. Before it is piped to the water main, it has to be filtered and treated.

water tower

storage tanks

reservoir

dam

pump

filtering and treatment works

pump

pipeline

water main

Electricity from water

Electricity is produced in power stations by large machines called **generators.** Generators must have a source of power such as coal or oil in order to work. One-sixth of all the electricity in the world is made in hydroelectric power stations, which use the power of falling water to drive the generators.

Falling water

Some hydroelectric power stations are built beside huge waterfalls. Pipes take water from the river above the waterfall, where the current is strong. The water rushes down the pipes into the power station where it forces the **turbines** that drive the generators to spin around and produce electricity. Power lines, held up by tall **pylons,** take the electricity from the power station to the cities and towns.

When there is no waterfall near the site of a power station, dams are used to make reservoirs instead and increase the force of the water rushing through the dam from the reservoir. The water is piped from the reservoir to the power station, which may be built as part of the dam. When the dam and the power station are a long distance apart, however, the water is carried from the reservoir in pipes or tunnels.

Inside the power station

The generators occupy a huge room in the power station. There is a turbine under the floor beneath each generator. The water from the reservoir rushes down through the pipes and hurls itself against the blades of the turbine. This make the blades spin around at high speed, turning the shaft that drives the generator. As the water leaves the turbine, it flows through more pipes until it reaches a river or lake beyond the power station.

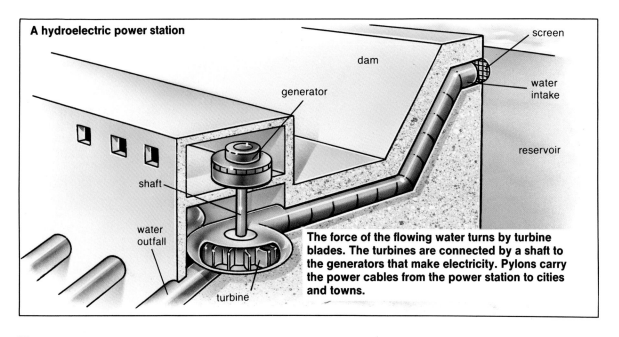

A hydroelectric power station

screen

dam

generator

water intake

reservoir

shaft

water outfall

turbine

The force of the flowing water turns by turbine blades. The turbines are connected by a shaft to the generators that make electricity. Pylons carry the power cables from the power station to cities and towns.

▲ Australia's Snowy Mountains hydroelectric scheme includes 16 dams and 7 power stations. All are overseen from a central control room.

Using the water again

Some hydroelectric power stations use the **pumped storage** method of using water over and over again. At night, when the demand for power is not very great, electricity is fed into the plant to operate the turbines, instead of water. The turbines work in reverse, pumping water from the river or lake back up the pipes to the reservoir. The electricity to operate the turbines comes from other power stations that work day and night.

The pumped storage method of producing electricity is inexpensive and does not waste water. It keeps the reservoir full, so that there is always enough water to make electricity during the day.

Make a turbine

You will need: a sheet of thin card four inches (ten centimeters) square, a large, wide drinking straw, scissors, some sticky tape, and a sink.

1 Fold the card in the four ways shown.

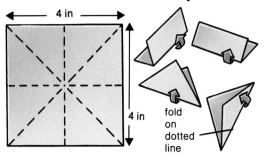

4 in

4 in

fold on dotted line

2 Make turbine blades from the card as shown. Hold the opposite corners of the card. Pinch them and, at the same time, push them inwards.

turbine blades

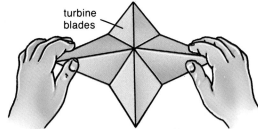

3 Make four cuts 3 inches (8 centimeters) long in one end of the straw. Fit the 4 turbine blades into the 4 cuts. Use sticky tape to bind the cut end of the straw together again.

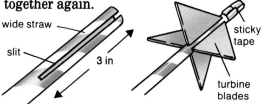

wide straw

slit

3 in

sticky tape

turbine blades

4 Put the turbine blades under cold running water. Rest the straw loosely in your hand so that it spins around freely. What happens if you increase or decrease the speed of the water? What happens if you change the position of the blades under the tap?

Sea power

The sea level along the coasts of seas and oceans rises and falls twice a day. These changes of sea level are called tides. In some parts of the world, the levels of high and low tide are vastly different.

Using the tides

In narrow bays and in the mouths of rivers, the water flows in as the tide rises and flows out again as the tide falls. It is possible, by damming the river, to make use of the moving water to generate electricity. This type of dam is called a **barrage.**

A barrage does not stop the water from flowing, but contains large pipes that let the water through. Inside the pipes are turbines, similar to those in hydroelectric power stations, which spin around as the tide flows in and out. They drive generators in the barrage that produce electricity.

The first tidal power station

So far, only one barrage has been built to make use of the tides. It is 2638 feet (804 meters) long, and it lies across the mouth of the Rance River in western France. There, the difference between the tides is about 33 feet (ten meters). Opened in 1966, this barrage is the world's first tidal power station.

The Rance Barrage is equipped with 38 turbines. These work even when the tidal water is not moving in or out. At such times, electricity is fed to the barrage to

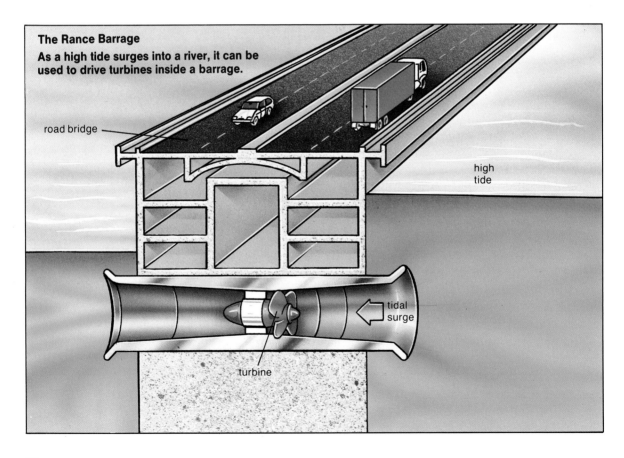

The Rance Barrage
As a high tide surges into a river, it can be used to drive turbines inside a barrage.

road bridge

high tide

tidal surge

turbine

make the turbines pump water from the sea into the river. This extra water flows back through the barrage later, as the tide goes out, producing more electricity when it is needed.

Everlasting power

Some sources of power get used up. Once oil and coal have been used to generate electricity, they cannot be used again. However, the tides provide a source of power that will last as long as the moon and sun last. After the cost of building the barrage has been met, the power costs very little to produce.

▲ Strong tides off the western coast of France made the Rance River the ideal site for a tidal barrage.

However, tidal power stations are costly to build and work well only where there is a big rise and fall in the tide. A second one is being built across the Bay of Fundy, on the border between Canada and the United States. There, the sea rises and falls as much as 56 feet (17 meters)—which is the biggest tide difference in the world. A third tidal power plant may be built across the Severn River in Britain.

Walls against water

People often build barriers to stop the sea or rivers from flooding the land. These are not built, like other dams, to control the water or use it for power. They are just walls of soil or rock built to safeguard the land against very high tides and rivers in flood.

Sea walls and river defenses are sometimes huge. High banks alongside rivers are called **levees.** Some levees form naturally from the mud left by flood waters on the river bank. Over the years, the mud builds up into a bank. More often they are built to keep flood water away from farmland and towns. High levees line the Mississippi River in the United States. There are 3700 miles (6000 kilometers) of levees, some of which extend along the rivers that flow into the Mississippi as well.

Below sea level

The Netherlands has battled with the sea throughout its history, because most of the country is below sea level and very flat. To protect themselves from the sea, the Dutch people have built strong sea walls called **dykes.**

In parts of the Netherlands, the people have gained land from the sea. In 1932, they built a dam 18.6 miles (30 kilometers) long across a large bay and began to drain the water out of the bay. Now, many thousands of people live there on large areas of farmland called **polders,** which were once under the sea. The drainage work will be finished by the year 2000, when the polders will cover an area of 925 square miles (2400 square kilometers).

The Delta Project

In 1953, floods on the Dutch coast caused the deaths of nearly 2000 people. A combination of high tides and strong

▲ Levees line the banks of the Mississippi River, the longest river in the United States. The high banks protect the surrounding land from flooding.

▲ A barrier has been constructed across the East Scheldt River in the Netherlands. The Delta Project now protects the coast from tidal floods.

▲ The total area of the Netherlands has increased over the years as Dutch engineers reclaim land from the sea. They build dykes around an area before draining it to form polders.

winds drove the sea into the river mouths, until the rivers burst their banks. To stop such a disaster from happening again, Dutch engineers started work on the Delta Project, which was completed in 1986.

The Delta Project sealed off the mouths of four big rivers. Dams were built across three of the rivers, but a dam on the fourth river, the East Scheldt, would have prevented the tide coming into the river mouth and threatened the birds, fish, and animals that live there. A barrier with gates was built instead. It is 5.6 miles (9 kilometers) long and has 62 steel gates. When the sea rises to danger level, the gates close and the barrier holds the sea back. At other times, the gates stay open to let the tides in and out of the river mouth.

Holding back water

You will need: a large plastic tray, sand, soil, stones, small pebbles or gravel, and some clay.

1 Build a dam across the middle of the tray, using the sand. Fill the area behind the dam with water. Does the sand dam hold back the water? Repeat the experiment with dams made from the stones, gravel, soil, and clay.

2 Which material do you think is the best at holding back water? Which is the easiest to use?

Protecting cities

Many of the world's largest cities are situated by the sea or on the banks of tidal rivers. Some of them are in danger of being flooded whenever high tides and strong winds raise the level of the sea.

Some cities have sea walls to hold back the sea, but others are busy ports and have to stay open to shipping. Special barriers can protect these cities from flooding. The world's biggest flood barrier is in London, England. A bigger one is to be built in Venice, Italy.

The Thames Barrier

The River Thames flows through the middle of London. On several occasions, sea water has surged up the river and caused flooding.

More than a million people live or work near the Thames. If the river overflowed, it would be a disaster. To prevent this, the Thames Barrier was built across the river in the part of London nearest to the sea. The barrier has gates that close and hold back the water if there is any danger of flooding. Ordinarily, the gates stay open for ships to pass through.

The barrier is 1706 feet (520 meters) long and has nine **piers,** which are like towers in the water. Ten gates are attached to the piers. In the middle of the barrier there are four large gaps 200 feet (61 meters) wide. Their gates lie flat on the river bed most of the time, while ships pass through. To close the gaps, the gates

▼ The Thames Barrier was opened in 1984. Its bow-shaped gates are made of steel and are rotated so that they lie on the river bed out of the way of ships when not in use.

rotate upwards to face the oncoming tide. Each gate is 66 feet (20 meters) high. The six smaller gates also open and close. The Thames Barrier can hold back tides up to about ten feet (three meters) above normal.

Venice and the sea

Venice is one of the most beautiful cities in the world. Its lovely old buildings and canals attract many visitors to the city. Venice, however, is built on low islands near the shore. It floods several times a year when there are high tides. The new barrier will prevent further flooding in the future, while allowing ships through. It will also let in enough water to change the water in the canals and keep the city clean.

▲ Flood waters in St. Mark's Square, Venice. Twenty years ago, there were disastrous floods in Venice that destroyed or damaged many of the city's treasures. The new barrier should prevent such destruction from taking place again.

▼ When flooding is likely, air-filled canisters will rise to an angle of 45 degrees. Waves will break against the barrier just like they do on a beach and protect the city of Venice.

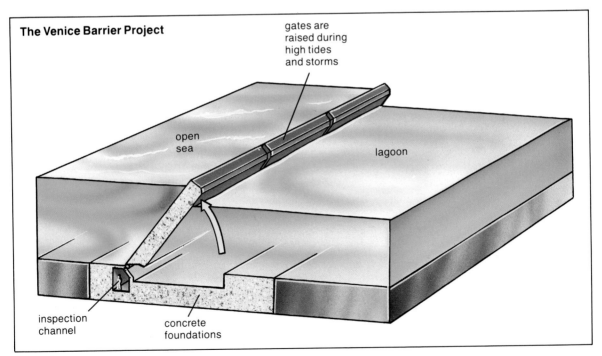

The Venice Barrier Project

gates are raised during high tides and storms

open sea

lagoon

inspection channel

concrete foundations

Dam disasters

Dam builders try to make sure that a dam is strong enough to hold back the water behind it, whatever happens. Sometimes, however, a dam breaks and the water roars down the valley, destroying everything in its path. The worst dam disaster ever recorded occurred at Morvi, in India, in 1979, when floods caused an earth dam to collapse. About 5000 people were killed.

A dam very seldom weakens but, if it does, there may be warning signs before it gives way. In that case, people can escape from danger. In 1976, the Teton Dam in Idaho, which was 312 feet (95 meters) high, collapsed. It had shown signs of weakness, and the actual dam burst was shown on television! Even so, 14 people died and there was millions of dollars worth of damage.

Shifting ground

Although a dam itself may be strong, the rock around it may not be able to support the dam and the water behind it. This was the case in Fréjus in France, in 1959. An arch dam collapsed when the rock in the valley sides gave way and more than 300 people died.

▼ When the Teton Dam burst, vast amounts of water and sand poured down the valley. Everything in the path of this flood was destroyed.

Earthquakes are a serious threat to dams. The shifting ground may no longer support the dam, or, as a reservoir fills with water, the weight of water on the ground may start an earthquake, which may damage or break the dam.

In 1963, the weight of water behind a high arch dam at Vaiont, in Italy, caused a landslide. The side of a mountain fell into the reservoir, producing a huge wave that rose 328 feet (100 meters) above the dam. The dam itself had the great strength of arch dams and did not burst. Nevertheless, about 2000 people were killed when the water from the reservoir flooded over the top of the dam.

▲ When the Machhu River Dam burst at Morvi, it left many thousands of people homeless as well as 5000 dead.

When a dam breaks

You will need: a hosepipe, some sand, and some water.

1 If possible, dam a stream of water on the beach.

2 Otherwise, use a large plastic tray and lay it on a flat surface outdoors. Build a dam across the middle with sand or soil. Use water from a hosepipe to fill the reservoir. When the water reaches the top make a small hole in the wall of the dam.

3 What happens when the water rushes through the hole in the dam? Why is so much damage done when a dam bursts?

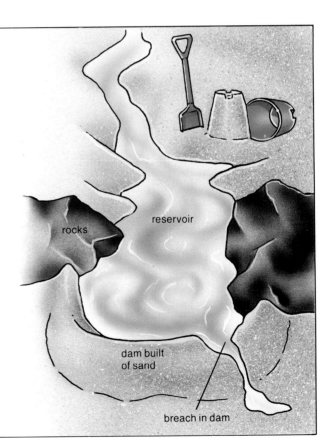

rocks

reservoir

dam built of sand

breach in dam

Problems

Dams play a vital part in our lives. They provide us with water and power and control floods. Yet some of the changes they bring are very unwelcome.

Houses, farms, and villages may have to be submerged when a dam is built, forcing the people who live there to move out and begin life somewhere else. Sometimes, fine buildings and ancient monuments are endangered. While the Aswan High Dam was being built in Egypt in 1968, the huge statues at the temple of Abu Simbel, built in about 1250 BC, had to be rescued from the rising waters of the reservoir, Lake Nasser.

Water changes

Some problems remain when a dam is finished. If a dam takes water from a river, the river below the dam will be affected. The water level will fall and people may no longer be able to travel along it by ship or catch fish in it.

Another problem is **silt,** which is the soil that is carried in the water of many rivers. As the river water flows into the reservoir, the silt settles to the bottom. As the reservoir fills with silt, it cannot store as much water as before. At the same time, water that has passed through the dam has lost some of its silt, which may have enriched the soil in the valley. In Egypt, the Nile River once flooded the plains every year, leaving its silt on the farmland. Since the Nile has been dammed, the soil is not so fertile.

Dams and wildlife

As a reservoir fills with water, it affects the creatures that live there. Most of the land animals can move away, but they sometimes get trapped and have to be rescued from islands that form in the reservoir.

Although the fish have plenty of water in which to swim, the dam may stop them from moving up and down the river. Some fish have to do this to survive. Salmon, for example, breed high up on the rivers. The young fish swim down to the sea. As adults, they return to the rivers and swim

◄ The temples and statues at Abu Simbel were built by the ancient Egyptians about 3000 years ago. Before the completion of the Aswan High Dam, the temples and statues were cut from the rock face. They were moved to a higher level above the rising waters.

▲ The Kariba Dam in Africa was built 30 years ago. As the level of the Zambezi River rose, thousands of wild animals had to be rescued and moved to safety.

▶ A dam may block the movement of fish up and down a river. Sometimes a fish ladder is built for the fish.

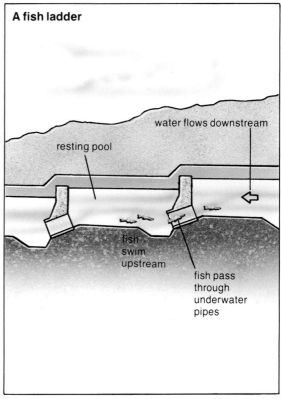

A fish ladder

water flows downstream

resting pool

fish swim upstream

fish pass through underwater pipes

up them again to breed. If they are stopped from doing this, the salmon cannot breed and will die.

One solution to this problem is to build a **fish ladder.** A fish ladder is a line of pools beside the dam, up which the fish can swim. There is also a fish lift, a special channel inside the dam, with gates that open to let the fish swim through.

Did you know?

▶ The Tarbela Dam is the largest dam in Pakistan and the largest earthfill dam in the world.

* The dam with the greatest volume is the New Cornelia Tailings Dam on the Ten Mile Wash in Arizona. It has a volume of 271 million cubic yards (209 million cubic meters). This earth dam, 98 feet (30 meters) high and 6.8 miles (11 kilometers) long, was completed in 1973.

* The biggest concrete dam in the world is the Grand Coulee Dam across the Columbia River in the State of Washington. It is a concrete gravity dam with a volume of 10.5 million cubic yards (8.1 million cubic meters) of concrete, and was completed in 1942. The Sayany Dam is a concrete arch-gravity dam now being built across the Yenisei River in the USSR. It will be the world's biggest dam when it is completed.

* The highest dam in the world is the Nurek Dam, built across the Vakhsh River in the USSR. It is an earth dam and is 984 feet (300 meters) high. The Nurek Dam was completed in 1986. The Rogunsky Dam is an earth dam now being built across the Vakhsh River. When it is completed, it will be 1099 feet (335 meters) high.

* The longest dam in the world today is the Yacyreta-Apipe Dam on the borders of Paraguay and Argentina in South America. It is 44.6 miles (72 meters) long.

▼ The Grand Coulee Dam blocks the Columbia River. It is only 548 feet (167 meters) high, but it holds back a reservoir 149 miles (240 kilometers) long.

* The largest reservoir in the world is the Kahkovskaya Reservoir in the USSR. The water in the reservoir has a volume of 113 cubic miles (182 cubic kilometers).

* The reservoir covering the largest area is in Africa. Lake Volta, in Ghana, has an area of 3275 square miles (8482 square kilometers). It is formed by Akosombo Dam, which was completed in 1965.

* The top three dam-building countries in the world are: the United States, with just over 5000 dams; Japan, with about 2000 dams; and India, with more than 1000 dams.

▲ The largest sea dam, completed 55 years ago, is Afsluitdijk Dam in the Netherlands. It is 18.6 miles (30 kilometers) long.

▼ Lake Volta now provides irrigation for Ghana's rice crop and livestock, hydroelectric power, and new fishing grounds.

Glossary

abutment: a part of a structure that is designed to withstand the force or weight of the part next to it.

arch dam: a dam that is curved like an arch. The ends of the arch take the strain and make the dam very strong.

barrage: any dam or platform built across a river to control or make use of its flow.

buttress dam: a straight concrete barrier that is supported by projecting walls, or buttresses.

chemical: a substance that reacts with another substance. Certain chemicals are used to kill germs in the water supply.

cofferdam: an enclosed barrier that keeps part of a site dry enough to work on while a dam is being built.

compress: to strengthen by squeezing together.

concrete dam: any kind of dam constructed from concrete. Concrete is made from cement, sand, stones, and water. The mixture hardens and becomes very strong.

core: the center of a dam, which may be made of clay and rocks.

cupola dam: a cupola is a shape like a dome. A cupola dam is a concrete barrier that curves like a dome. It is very strong.

cut-off: the layer of a dam that is built below the ground. It seals off any water that might seep underneath the dam.

dyke: an embankment raised to protect low-lying land from a sea or lake.

earth dam: a dam constructed from layers of soil or rock.

embankment dam: a broad, sloping dam made of soil or rock.

engineer: a person who makes use of scientific ideas in order to build structures, mines, or machines, or to work with chemicals or electricity.

filter: any device through which a liquid or gas is passed in order to remove solid matter or dirt.

fish ladder: a series of pools around the edge of a dam. A fish ladder allows salmon to bypass the dam and so return to their breeding waters.

flood barrier: a barrier across a river that can be raised before high tides or storm.

form: a wooden casing used as a mold to shape concrete as it hardens.

generator: a machine for making electrical power.

geologist: a scientist who studies rocks and soil.

gravity dam: a concrete barrier that holds back water because of its weight.

hydroelectric power: electric power which in generated by using fast-flowing water.

irrigate: to bring water to farmland by building channels from a lake, river, or reservoir.

levee: a high bank alongside a river.

piers: the parts of a flood barrier that support the gates.

polder: an area of land that was once covered by a sea or lake. The water has been drained away and kept back by high tides.

power station: a large building where electricity is made.

pumped storage: a method of supplying water to power stations during the night.

pylon: a steel mast carrying electrical cables overhead.

reservoir: a pool in which water is collected for use by people.

riprap: the layer of broken stones that covers one side of an embankment dam.

rockfill dam: a barrier made of rocks and sealed with clay or concrete.

silt: soil carried along by currents of water. It sinks to the bottom of seas and rivers, or is washed up on land by tides and floods.

sluice: a channel or pipe that can be opened or closed to control the flow or water.

spillway: a channel that carries away water from a reservoir if it is in danger of spilling over a dam.

stressed concrete: concrete that has been strengthened with steel rods or cables.

survey: to inspect closely, taking measurements.

turbine: a wheel that has many curved blades. It is turned by water or gas. Turbines drive machines that make electricity.

water authority: a group of people who organize the supply of water on behalf of a government, a council, or a company.

Index